Words for Teachers & Caregivers

in Small Doses

Words for Teachers & Caregivers

in Small Doses

JUDITH FRIZLEN

Book design and composition by Chelsea Cloeter
Cover art by Dasha Nadolinski

Published by
LifeWays North America
1515 W. Main St.
Norman, OK 73069

To purchase a copy of this book, go to www.lifewaysnorthamerica.org.

ear Readers,

Everyone who interacts with young children is a teacher. This includes child caregivers, parents and neighbors. This list also includes grocers, crossing guards and mail carriers.

Wherever we are and whatever we are doing, young children are watching and imitating our words, gestures and inner attitudes. It's an awesome responsibility to be human and to live in community. We are called to develop ourselves continually, to be not only teachers, but also lifelong students.

The best way to develop ourselves is with consistent practice. Just like the physical body responds to regular exercise, healthy eating habits and general care, so do our minds and souls. By reading an excerpt that inspires thought on a weekly basis, we can awaken and nurture aspects of ourselves. The rhythm of the action increases the benefits and decreases uncertainty of whether we will find time to do it or not. There is a plan.

When we hold a question in our thoughts, we are more likely to come across answers. The question acts as a filter for information coming in, sifting out what is relevant. Finding our own answers to questions ensures meaningful learning and increases confidence in our ability to learn from life's experience.

Studying and developing in community compounds the power of the activity, for we have much in common with our fellow humans. What is individual is also universal. The fabric of our lives is unique, with shared threads of humanity woven throughout.

The core of learning is to know your Self. On that foundation, develop your Self. Ask questions. Seek answers. Live fully and trust experience to be your guide. Remember that within each of us lives a child, regardless of our age.

I have been a teacher and parent for over thirty years and still have much to learn. Whatever I have learned, I want to give away. Isn't that the purpose of learning it? I look forward to sharing these thoughts and questions with you. May they serve you and your community well.

Judith Frizlen, Author and Founder of
The Rose Garden Early Childhood Center
Buffalo, New York

Contents

Autumn

Winter

Spring

Summer

JULY

AUGUST

AUTUMN

Returning Home

ℱIRST SEPTEMBER WEEK

The cool morning air tells us that autumn is coming. The light is golden and there is mist in the air. Spider webs glisten in the sunshine and the morning dew.

Summer gave herself fully to us and now she is withdrawing. Autumn is slowly calling nature to go to sleep for the winter. In preparation, plants go to seed and we gather the harvest and begin the process of settling the garden. The days are still fair; we savor these final days of summer's warmth and sweetness.

How do you support the transition from one season to the next?

We witness nature turning inward and we do, too. We count our blessings like fruits of the harvest in our basket. Look at what we have been given; we store the memory of the mellow summer days and hold them in our hearts so we will stay warm in the months ahead.

Second September Week

Summer's expansiveness has a sanguine mood; imagine a butterfly in the air. In this mood, we can flit from one activity, one thought to another with ease. When September comes, that mood is replaced by a light-filled focus that shows us our goals. The strength of our soul forces enters our will, and with the strength of that focus, we are shown the way.

Like a lantern that lights up the next step, the radiant glow we carry within at summer's end allows us to bring light into the darkness of forging a new path. When we do so, we know we are on our way, we are on the path. The goals we hold in mind focus our awareness, and the light within shows us the next step. The goal may be distant at first; with the guiding light, we move toward it, one step at a time. The light of trust and the knowledge that we can do what we set out to do will lead us to the goal.

Find your goals. Nourish the light within. Step out boldly to do what is yours to do. Your efforts will bear good fruit.

What are your goals?

THIRD SEPTEMBER WEEK

Nature is drawing inward, the plants and animals are preparing for their winter's rest. Humans at this time are also going inward, but rather than preparing to sleep, we are invited to wake up. The divine work of humankind will happen in the dark months ahead. In the transition toward inwardness, we turn away from the externals to find what lives deep within us, to sow seeds of the divine. Now that it is getting colder and darker outside, we must rely on our own forces. Our will is shaped by our goals and intentions; our heart is warmed by our feelings, and our spirits are connected to our thoughts.

As we reach into our depths, we rise to our heights. Like the tall tree that stands sturdy because its roots stretch deep into the earth, the human capacity to rise up is supported by our ability to go deeply within. Reach for the depths within and you will know your strength, your capacity to connect with the heavenly grace and to do what has been given to you to do.

What inner resources support you in achieving your goals?

15

Throughout the warm summer days, we were nurtured by Mother Nature and her many gifts. Now it is time to let the fire of the sun and the warmth in our hearts find expression through our will. It is strong and can be a force for good in the world when that is our desire.

At the autumn equinox, we might pause to find a sense of balance. The hours of day and night have evened out; this beckons us to notice, to attend to the harmony in nature while she slowly transitions from summer to fall, from light to darkness, from warm to cold, from active growth upward to resting close and within the earth. Humans are transitioning, too.

How do you cultivate kindness?

When our inward focus grows, awareness brings us the information we need to grow in our humanity. We notice when we are outside of ourselves, and we can then take time to find our strength within. Deep inside each one of us are the answers to our questions. Notice thoughts, feelings and physical sensations. Be aware of what is going on inside, so you can discern what is yours and what belongs to others. In the summertime, we connect outwardly with ease; in the wintertime, we must consciously bring our best out into the world, finding compassion in our relationships with our self and others. Be a witness to all this.

$\mathcal{F}$IFTH SEPTEMBER WEEK

Michaelmas Day is a celebration of the harvest. Knowing that now that her work is done, Mother Nature is getting ready to go to sleep. Simultaneously, the human soul awakens and we prepare to go on an inward journey through the dark and cold days ahead. Michaelmas season begins September 29th and extends through the winter solstice. St. Michael is known as the provider of courage and strength to fight evil. Pictures show him on a white horse with an iron sword used to vanquish the dragon. With that sword, he cast Lucifer out of Heaven.

At this time, acknowledging that we have our own dragons to vanquish, we may choose to set a personal development goal. Some examples are: listen better, increase patience, or be kinder to ourselves and others. With that intention in mind, we notice our behavior and our thoughts about our behavior. Then we can continue striving to reach the mark that we set for ourselves.

Aside from the inner development aspect of this festival, we often gather in community to celebrate the harvest, to be nourished and strengthened by friendship and harvest bread. When both the outward and inward expressions of the season come together to give us what we need, we enter Michaelmas time ready for the journey.

What are your intentions for Michaelmas time?

While it is becoming darker and colder outside, the sun will live in our souls for safekeeping until we release it back to nature in the springtime. When we nurture the sun's power within us, it gives us strength in our will, strength in our soul and strength in our spirit. Strength in our soul and spirit involve not only confidence but humility. We must learn about our strengths but also refrain from avoiding knowledge of our weaknesses. A common habit is to pay attention to the faults of others rather than recognizing and working on our own; this does not assist us in meeting self-development goals.

While tapping into heavenly power, we can keep the ground under our feet by striving for honesty. We are aware that ideals are for us to seek but never to achieve. We all make mistakes and can always strive again, but cannot expect to achieve perfection. In lieu of perfection, Rudolf Steiner suggested that we bring enthusiasm, which will take us a long way toward our goals.

On a path of self-development, it is through meeting what we fear that we develop courage. When we are able to see what lives in the shadows and bring it into the light, we develop the courage, confidence and calm necessary to meet life's challenges. Everyone experiences challenges and knows both darkness and light; that is our shared humanity. How we meet the challenges that come our way is the means for developing our full human potential.

Where do you find courage in meeting challenges?

SECOND OCTOBER WEEK

To meet the dark and cold days ahead takes strength. Where can we find it? While our experience of life is unique and personal, there is a universal component: It is through our connection with the universal that we are strengthened.

According to physical law, things contract with the cold, and this state can trigger fearfulness in humans, causing constriction in our bodies, minds and souls. It can also be accompanied by feelings of separation and loneliness. When constricted and fearful, we know we have lost our power and with it, our confidence. It is as if we are trying to slay the dragon without the mighty sword of steel seen in depictions of Michael.

What is your strength?

We can release constriction and overcome fear with love; it warms our hearts, availing us of its mighty forces. Through love, we connect with our higher self and are armed with the warmth of the Light, the light of the sun. Love is generated by action, and taking action with the intention of expressing love helps generate feelings of love for ourselves, our fellow humans and for Life itself. The feelings of constriction are released and we grow confident, armed with the power of love and of light. When we give love, it grows in us and all around us, giving us strength.

THIRD OCTOBER WEEK

When we tend the spark of light in our hearts, the fire within us grows. At times, it is a small flame that warms us within, granting a quiet strength. There are times when it is a raging fire that spurs us on to express our truth even in the face of disagreement, or to engage in a difficult task. Whether the flame burns big or small, it is always bright. How do we keep the fire burning within when the light outside ourselves is dwindling? We nurture the flame with warm thoughts, with humor, with song and with a willingness to work. If we resist what must be done, the light grows dim.

In the autumn, there is work in preparing our outdoor and indoor spaces for the coming winter. Outside, we harvest what is left in the garden and we may cover the beds with straw. Then we store away anything that cannot endure the harsh weather ahead.

Inside our homes, we prepare our spaces for more indoor time. Removing clutter and cleaning our environment with care are ways that allow the forces of nature (often referred to as elementals) to support us in creating order. If we ignore the forces of nature, they wreak havoc; they create the feeling of chaos that we can see and experience when we enter an untended room. Although cobwebs in the corner and dust bunnies under the chair may seem small, they have an energy that can become negative unless it is brought into the service of human endeavor. We do so by putting things where they belong and by wiping a wet cloth over surfaces and in the corners. Children respond to our efforts to address the forces of nature. As with anything that is lurking in the shadows, when we bring it into the light and clean it up, we free up energy for what we are choosing to create, we rein in forces that may be otherwise stuck. Conduct your own experiments with this: Tend your indoor space with care and then notice the effect on you.

Do you tend your home with care?

FOURTH OCTOBER WEEK

The trees in autumn give us the ripened fruit we love to eat. Just as the summer sun makes the autumn fruit strong and sweet, the inner work we do in winter bears fruit that will ripen in the springtime. That fruit will be strong and sweet in time. Just as fruit trees are vulnerable to frost in the late springtime, our souls may be vulnerable during this late autumn time. It is time to accept what is, hone our focus on what we seek, and to let go of what we do not need for the journey ahead.

Remember what makes us strong and sweet is the challenges we meet. Just as the apple grows strong on the tree when it faces the elements in nature, we grow strong too, when we face what comes toward us. We can withstand the wind, rain and cold. We can withstand the misunderstandings, mistakes and relationship challenges; we can learn, grow, and forgive. We can stay awake and aware by practicing objectivity and care. With confidence and humility, we can ask for help from forces beyond the material realm and remember that ultimately everyone (including ourselves) is seeking love and understanding. It might not appear that way, but the truth is that, on a soul level, we are all seeking love and understanding. Give it to yourself and each other and you will find that the fruits of your efforts will grow ripe, strong and sweet, and you will live in the garden of your own making.

Do you give to others what you would like to receive?

When we nurture the light within us, little by little its power grows. With time we may notice that our efforts to strengthen the fire begin to inspire our actions. We may find that our hearts are filled with joy, that we feel stronger, that our light can be a force that helps heal hurt and sadness in others.

Kindness, good deeds and reflection support the light within. At the end of each day and the end of each week, look back on what happened, investigate your own life. Consider whether the light within was shining through in your interactions. When we acknowledge when and where the fire burned brightly through our deeds and the deeds of others, we can learn to master that flame. We can do what will support it.

Does the light you share come back to you?

The light will grow when we share it. If we keep it to ourselves, it stays small. Notice the light that comes from others and express gratitude for it. Through our awareness, acknowledgement and heartfelt striving, we can keep the light burning within. That light that will keep us warm throughout the winter and reflect its power back toward us through our community.

When we find inspiration, it lightens our thoughts, making them nimble and uplifted. Inspired thoughts kindle a feeling of warmth in our hearts. We may also experience strengthening of our will and, with it, energy or bounce in our step. Notice how important inspiration is for our well-being and our ability to be effective in the world!

We must seek the light to create a vessel for inspiration or breath to enter our bodies, souls and minds. That searching begins with clear intentions, an open mind and an open heart. With this engagement, inspiration can be revealed to us. When we are filled with the light, we are able to meet all that comes in the world, including darker, shorter days. We find the courage to face life without fear.

At this time of year, when each day is a little shorter and darker, we may recognize a feeling of heaviness, of darkness. We can then choose to search for the light in uplifting readings, rituals and human connections. The lantern walk at Martinmas is one ritual to celebrate the light within; it leaves an imprint that lingers in our souls and our community long after the festival.

What inspires you?

We do not need to understand everything that comes to us. Sometimes our thinking is not enough. It might reinforce thoughts that are limiting, that are not serving us. Yet when our thinking is spiritually imbued or enlightened, it takes us beyond the personal realm into what is universal, to that which encompasses all that is and all that will be. This brings us back to the personal and what we can do. Seek inspiration.

The golden leaves still clinging onto branches and covering the ground will slowly disappear, the ground will freeze and the landscape will become gray and empty. This is nature's time to rest.

While nature rests, humans are awake. This is the time of year that we recall the power of our humanity that will carry us through the winter months. Remember the light and bright lanterns we held during the Martinmas festival and the story of Martin, the soldier who shared his cloak with a beggar who was shivering in the cold. Generosity warms the hearts of both giver and receiver. The more we give, the more we are given.

As we embrace our inner power at this time of year, we may also notice a twinge of discomfort while we let go of the outer light and enter the darkness. By letting discomfort into our awareness, we allow it to move through us. Just as gracefully as the trees let go of their leaves, we too can experience and release our emotions. In this way, we connect to our souls and fellow humans as we reach out to each other for support.

Have you created a container for the light within?

By connecting to inner personal realms and to others, we find comfort and strength. Through our human efforts of thinking, feeling and doing, we can connect to what is and tend to the rifts that need healing. The world needs each of us to perform our tasks and to create a container for the light until spring comes again.

When we are afraid, angry or troubled, these human emotions trigger a physiological response that ensures our survival. But in survival mode, the range of options narrows, veiling responses unrelated to the immediate threat. We cannot access our best thinking and are prone to reactivity.

Most problems we encounter do not actually challenge our survival, although they might trigger emotional discomfort. Become aware of what is happening within and do what is necessary to maintain access to your best thinking and decision-making capabilities.

But how to disrupt the survival state once triggered? Physical activity is good; it engages the will and enlivens the body. Focusing on gratitude is beneficial; it awakens the heart forces. It generates positivity and joy, which are then self-perpetuating. Cultivate an attitude of gratitude. Celebrate Thanksgiving and give thanks for all we have been given. Remember that when something comes along that triggers uncomfortable emotions, it does not take away what we have to be grateful for, although it may cloud our thinking or hide our awareness of those gifts. When we remember what we have been given, we can maintain an awareness, an attitude that allows gratitude to grow and with it, the gifts of contentment, peace and hopefulness.

What fruits does gratitude bear?

Seeking Light

FIRST DECEMBER WEEK

I am given a job to do, one that serves both the world and me when I do it well. If I do what is mine to do, I am filled with the strength I need and the light that comes with fulfilling it. While we are waiting and anticipating the return of the light in nature, one of our tasks is to go inward and reflect.

During the weeks prior to the winter holiday, we can prepare ourselves to receive the light. In the Christian tradition, this period is referred to as Advent. The first week is a time of honoring the physical body as represented by stones, shells and bones. Take time during this week to recollect anything that came to you in the physical form during the past year.

Are you aware of what your physical body needs?

Take care of your physical body in special ways, too. Give it rest, good nourishment and care. Listen to what it is telling you, for it can be a bearer of great wisdom. One of the ways we can honor our physical bodies is to move forward consciously without rushing. Winter is the ideal time for slowing down even while there are many holiday related activities that call to us. Ironically, the best way to arrive anywhere on time and ready is to slow down and pay attention both inwardly and outwardly along the way. Although the natural world is dark and the trees are bare, the Light will return; be ready!

Look back over the year that is ending and consider your habits. In the tradition of Advent, during the second week, we are recognizing our etheric bodies. This is the body that we have in common with the plant world; we can take in food, process it and grow. Our nourishment comes in many forms. It comes in the form of the food we eat, in the form of the sensory information we take in, and in the form of the thoughts and feelings we hold. Our ability to process what we take in depends on both what we choose to ingest and how our system's internal climate receives it, both of which are impacted by our habits.

Consider your current habits or life practices. Do you continually do something that perpetuates difficulty for you? An example is waking up without enough time to prepare for the day, so having to rush and perhaps often arriving late and in a state of stress. If you recognize a habit that is not serving you, consider a change.

What are your habits?

It takes practice and patience to change a habit. We cannot expect overnight success and even when we start out well, slips can happen. Avoid punishing yourself when they do, for this is not an effective method to achieve positive results and you might create instead a self-fulfilling prophecy limiting your growth. When an old habit reappears, recommit to your goal to learn a new habit and start again. Little by little, one habit and one day, sometimes one hour at a time, we can change even longstanding habits. As humans, we all have the ability to learn and to change.

Entering the third week of Advent, we continue to prepare for the return of the Light. When we consider the qualities of young children, it is not difficult to imagine the Light returning in the form of a child as it does in the Christian tradition. Looking into the face of a young child is like watching the sun rise, a wonder to behold when you stop and really look!

This is the week to consider our emotional life and our instincts. In our astral bodies, we have correspondences to the animal world. A dog is loyal and programmed to greet people whenever they come through the door. A cat can detect sorrow in a human being and know to come and sit in a lap to provide comfort. These are not conscious choices, but rather innate sensibilities.

We too, have sensibilities that allow us to feel the emotions of another, in a room and certainly, in ourselves. Take time to consider your emotions and your relationships, beginning with the one with yourself. How do you relate to your emotions? Are you a slave to them or disconnected from them? Either extreme leads to imbalance, for emotions provide information, but they are only a piece of the picture, they are not facts. They can show up in our lives much like a young child, tugging at our leg to get our attention. We can acknowledge them, label them, and still choose in freedom what we are going to think and do. While humans have some things in common with the animal kingdom, we also have a power that takes us beyond the animal world and links us with the angelic realm.

Do you allow emotional information to inform but not dictate your life?

It is time for the return of the Light. We are ready to consider what completes our humanity. In each human being, there is a bit of the divine and, with it, the capacity for pure love.

As human beings living on the earth, we are connected to the animal kingdom. But with our thinking, we can access the spiritual world, the heavenly realms. During this time of year, when we celebrate the return of the Light, there is an opening, a portal for us to enter and meet the divine. When we have prepared our bodies, souls and minds for this experience, we can more fully reap the benefits.

Picture your ideals, your highest aspirations and your connection to spiritual support. Strengthen your knowledge of this realm and your ability to connect to it. Where do you find this connection? Many find it in holiday rituals, both social and personal. Giving from the heart is one way we feel our divine connection. The spirit of the holiday is captured in the practice of giving and receiving, inspired by realms that we might visit but will not live in as long as we are on the earthly plane. The divine is eternal, our human experience is not. When we live by our highest ideals, we expand into divine realms and the timeline of eternity. Celebrate the return of the Light and the divine that is in you and in me; watch and wait for it to become visible now and throughout the coming year.

What is your highest purpose?

In the heart there dwells
in bright radiance
our helping sense.

In the heart there works
in warming power
our helping strength.

So may we bear
the soul's full will
into heart warmth,
into heart light;

So may we bring
healing to those
who need healing
through God's sense of grace.

—RUDOLF STEINER

Meditation for Courage and Tranquility
Sophia Books, Forest Row, UK:
Rudolf Steiner Press, 2002

It's a new day, a new season, a new year! If you took time to renew yourself and review the past year, you may feel refreshed and alive with possibility. Like a fresh blanket of snow, the new year awaits our footprints. It is new and innocent like a child. It is tender and precious like a rose, ready to unfold. What do we want to bring to this new year? How do we want to be in it? Are we able to choose or will we follow unconscious patterns that drive us to react rather than respond to situations?

What are your questions?

If you have not yet reflected on the past year and the one to come, you might not have answers, but then again, reflection often brings us to the questions, and the answers come later. Defining the questions is a great start. Ask the questions, then let go to allow the answers to come, while you wait in quiet anticipation. Inspirational thoughts, like snowflakes, come to us as unique and precious gifts that seem to fall from the sky. Receive them with the open wonder of a child.

When the holidays are over, we have a warm afterglow and the coldest days of winter. Filled with the warmth of gatherings, gift-giving and sweet treats, we are ready to face them. We have celebrated the light and we are starting our journey toward spring with a little more light each day, while still in the midst of the darkness, the grayness, and the cold of winter. Winter is the season that turns us inward toward our souls to find peace and comfort.

What seeds are germinating in your soul?

There is no relief in winter by complaining or blaming; that will only make it harder to get through it. Nature will do what nature does, and it is up to us to follow her cue. Everything in nature is resting; it is not time for great spurts in outward growth. We too can slow down to rest our bodies, minds and souls at this time.

Our thoughts, just like the seeds and bulbs underground and the buds on the trees, are unseen, germinating.

In the spring, they will sprout. If we are unaware of what we are nourishing in our thinking, our souls and our deeds, we will find out when they break ground, even poking up out of the snow in early spring, saying, "Look at me, I am here and ready to grow." Stop and pay attention to your thoughts, for they will not remain invisible for long; the plants we seed in our minds will grow, making apparent what we have been nourishing. Let winter's inward stillness bring you to gifts of quiet self-awareness and acceptance that will bloom later in your spring garden.

The journey from the autumn equinox to the winter solstice is one of anticipation, awaiting the return of the light. We set personal intentions for Michaelmas time to strengthen our will forces while entering this time of darkness. If the path from autumn equinox to the spring equinox were a tunnel with light on either end, we would be past the halfway mark. Each day stretches a bit longer and brings us closer to the end of winter.

Although we are drawn inward by the season, balance is important so we brace ourselves against the cold and go outside to engage in cold-weather activities. We cannot spend all of winter on the couch; our muscles would languish and so would our souls; we would grow restless. It's time to skate, ski, snowshoe or just trudge through the snow. It takes a measure of bravery to step out into the cold, to negotiate the snowy and sometimes icy walkways, to use our physical strength to meet the elements. After being out in the cold, we are grateful for the warmth and comfort of home. Our tired bodies welcome warm food or drink and rest.

There is also the constant strength of our heart forces, although we might need to fan their flames in winter with a playful spirit. Play is the vehicle for development of the child, and it is essential for adults as well. It is a way to restore ourselves, release stress, and find the world anew. Watch children in the winter, then consider making a snow angel or snow fort or sledding down the hill along with them. If you see the world through the eyes of a child, cleaning the snow off the car can be a wonder! Flakes might sparkle and fly or stick to the windshield with icy resolve. It is time to move, to play, and to appreciate the wonder of the elements while we journey forward to the light at the end of the tunnel.

How do you express your playful spirit?

What a difference it makes to generate our own heat rather than rely on outside sources! When we can produce light and heat with our own heart forces, we have found a deep source of power within ourselves. Ice and frost outdoors are not likely to go away soon, but when we meet winter elements with the warmth of fire, our heart becomes a hearth. It is fire that transforms ice into water and then to air, new elements altogether.

Besides playful activity, heart forces can be sparked by our own thoughts and warm human interactions. Try this experiment: A smile often elicits a smile. Pausing to share information about food, the weather or work allows a simple errand to transform into a heart-warming encounter with another. For example, this morning, the check-out clerk at the supermarket shared his breakfast menu and the importance of good nutrition. Where did you learn this? I asked him. He told me it was from his mother and sister and that childhood is the time to form good eating habits. Words I could have spoken myself, I thought, but hearing them from someone else was a bonus, a warm human connection that remained with me all the while I put groceries into the trunk of my car and yet still as I sit at my desk writing. See for yourself if the spark of warmth from a smile, a verbal exchange, or a kind deed fuels the fire of heart forces, preventing wintery ice from forming.

What warms your heart in winter?

In addition to accepting what is happening outside in the winter, we might notice it's a challenge to keep our temperament in balance. The extreme difference between indoor and outdoor temperatures, and the demands of going back and forth between them can set our bodies and souls off kilter.

Each of us carries the four elements of water, earth, air and fire within. However, one of them will predominate, two more are secondary and the fourth one is our weak spot. If you lack fire in winter, you might find that you feel sluggish. You might need to cultivate this element in your soul. What sparks your life force? What brings you joy?

Do you stoke your inner hearth?

What speaks to your soul? This is important to know and to consciously go toward. Depending on your temperament and the element you lead with, your fire will look different.

You might bake something new, wear a warm color or contact an old friend. On the other hand, you might cross country ski (that will warm you up!) or drink hot chocolate or memorize a poem. It is important to know who we are so when the seasons hold sway, we know which element to shore up on. Finding your fire keeps you connected to the sun in the midst of the dark winter. Feet on the earth, we connect with the heavens.

The Candlemas festival on February 2nd is a celebration of the return of the light and with it, rumblings in the cold dark ground and rebirthing of the green world. Long before we see spring flowers, something starts happening under the ground. From above, heavenly light reawakens activity in the earth at this time of year midway between the winter solstice (the shortest day and longest night) and the spring equinox (when day and night are equally long).

Regardless of outdoor temperatures and weather conditions, the rhythmic changes in light are cause for celebration, for dipping candles that we can use year round, according to tradition. When we make candles, the smell of the golden beeswax fills the air and reminds us of the warmth of summer. The slow and steady process of dipping the wick into a pot of molten wax builds both a candle and patience. Yes, spring and all its glory will come, but not overnight. The light will return a little bit at a time; we cannot rush it. We can trust, though, that it happens every year, in spite of high winds and changeable weather.

Encouraged by nature's cycles, we can choose to allow the light of the sun to illuminate our human consciousness and renew our thinking. Much like what is happening in the earth, we can notice a reawakening also in our physical bodies and allow what's green and growing to bloom in our hearts and souls. What stirrings do you feel in your mind, body and soul at this time of the year? How can you consciously celebrate the light, trusting, accepting, and patiently awaiting the slow and steady process of its return?

Do you acknowledge the gradual return of the light?

With winter's final stretch before us, darkness persists and dragons may lurk. They may frighten us if we have not yet recognized them for what they are. We may be challenged to be our best self, to stand upright and remain sound. We can find strength by looking back at the celebration of the light in deep winter, the light that returned in the form of a child. In the brightness of that moment, the beauty and innocence of the child evokes wonder and reverence.

This radiant light brings clarity and with it the ability to see things as they are, to name them. According to Rudolf Steiner, there are two ways to address dragons or evil: recognition and humor. For example, when I know what is happening inside of me, I am better able to see things as they are without filling in the blanks, to look back and note where reality ends and my own fabrications begin. Once we see things as they are, they may lose their power to make us afraid. If we can add humor to the situation, we can release tightness and open up to possibilities. The physical act of laughing changes our breathing and with it our inner chemistry.

How do you cultivate a sense of humor?

We may not find the answers to our questions immediately, but we might feel more comfortable in the not knowing once we identify what we *do* know. While we walk in the darkness, the light of consciousness reveals our next step, and although we may not know where the path will lead us, we do know where we are in the moment. A vision of where we are headed guides us. Darkness will lessen, spring will come. Unknowns will become known and we may choose to walk in knowledge of what is, with trust and humor.

The earth is the Mother of all living things. She leads us to rebirth at this time of year. With this growth there is joy, renewed strength, and a sense of the magic of life. Before long, in the dark, wet earth, tiny plants will pop up through the snow. Before this birth, we prepare ourselves by deep cleaning both inside and outside. What is new must be held in a pure and fresh container.

We often see nature tables at this time of year with a form of Lady Spring in the air or on the ground with a broom in hand to clean up winter's debris. Just as nature is preparing for rebirth, we are preparing for it in our homes and in our hearts. Many traditions involve dietary cleanses and deep house-cleaning. In the tradition I grew up in, we would strengthen our will by letting go of some-thing we liked during the forty days before Easter. It was easy to give up something that we did not care for, but the idea was to let go of something we *did* care for, and meet-ing that challenge would strengthen us. Chocolate was popular to give up since we knew our Easter baskets would be filled with it which would more than make up for the weeks of for-feit.

Aside from habits of consumption, we can choose to let go of any behaviors that no longer serve us. That conscious-ness opens up the possibility of breaking habits and allowing new behaviors to grow in our lives. Hence, the rebirth in Mother Earth is a moment of reawakening in humans if we allow the Mother of all living things to be our guide.

Is there a habit you would like to release?

FOURTH FEBRUARY WEEK

Sunlight is returning; it is apparent. It streams through the atmosphere, warming the earth and filling our souls. At sunrise, the rays pierce through the darkness, banishing the night. Throughout the day, the warm rays melt the snow, cause icicles to drip and puddles to form.

The young child is often compared to springtime, full of exuberant, fresh and radiant light. You can see it in their faces. Springtime is considered the morning of the year, just as early childhood is the morning of our lives. It is from love that children are born and in the springtime, there is a reawakening of Love in the form of Light. It is the season when we find the power to reconnect with others after the inward nature of winter.

How does the warmth of the sun live in your soul?

Rudolf Steiner said, "We can find Nature outside us only if we have first learned to know her within us." When the light and love of springtime live in our souls, we can truly know the experience of nature. We share that knowledge with young children through our gaze. Looking with eyes of love, we reflect the warmth and light of the sun.

When children experience human warmth, they feel welcome and grow secure in a world that is good. The adult's loving gaze, reliable as the sun that rises every day, can support children in becoming the unique human beings latent within them. When we awaken these human forces, seeds of humanity grow and develop.

SPRING

*M*aintaining Balance

When the light returns in spring, the sap flows upward in the trees and plants peek up out of the ground. That life force bubbles up in us too, waking us from winter's darkness and stillness. It can also lead to a feeling of disturbance or instability. To balance the strong forces that reawaken in the spring, we need to find the ground under our feet and keep our thoughts illuminated by what is true.

Emerging from the darkness into the light gives us strength; but where there is light, there is also darkness and, therefore, shadows. We must get to know the shadows, for they can block the light. If we find ourselves in a state of overexcitement or loss of hope, perhaps we are standing in a shadow. This is the time of year to search for the light, to emerge from the darkness and to welcome the dawn of the year; but this can be unsettling.

In the light's brilliance, we find knowledge of our higher self and how things truly are, brimming with possibility. Experiencing the hopefulness of spring as a guiding force, we need to stand strong and not become unbalanced, ungrounded or unaware. There is a certain comfort in the womblike darkness of winter, so waking from winter's sleep might be startling, as if we are coming out of a dream. In spite of the shadows, imagine we could step into the light with confidence, with hope and with courage. What would we have to release? Who would we be then?

Do you meet both light and shadow with courage?

There are basic elements: earth, air, fire and water. There are organic processes involving the elements that bring them into movement or to life. Leave a cup of water out on the ledge and you will see algae grow in it. Some cultures (Irish for one) personify these processes by calling them nature spirits or elementals, and you will often find them in children's art and literature. These little characters will either support the work of humans or wreak havoc, depending on how we treat them. Even without the ability to see them, it is not farfetched to imagine that there are small unseen entities that bring our attention to the life force in elements and appeal to children (or adults) who live in the realm of imagination.

I am sure you have heard of the earth elementals called gnomes. They work with the ground and soil. In the realm of air, we have sylphs that are often associated with flowers and trees. You can picture their work as integral to the health and beauty of growing things. Salamanders are in the realm of fire and their job is to cleanse or purge. We also often speak of sun or light fairies in the specks of dust that show up when light shines through them. Water fairies called undines are associated with bodies of water. Imagine a flowing stream and the fairies working to help the water move over and around the rocks or the tides to ebb and flow in oceans and lakes. You may also consider the impact of garbage, toxic chemicals, or other human carelessness on the work of elementals.

Although I have never seen an elemental, I have experienced the effects of working with the processes of nature, ignoring them, or worse yet, going against them. Their power is aligned with that of humans in that they augment the effects of our actions. For example, when we clean a space even getting the dirt out of the corners, we find that it stays clean, whereas when we allow the dirt to accumulate unattended, we find the dirt and dust grow. Consider the value of the elementals, strive to gain their assistance to lighten our work and maybe add a sense of magic.

Have you considered forces of nature or elementals?

During the transition from winter to spring, the element of air makes itself known in the wind. Winds of change blow and bring about changes in temperature, in the sky and even in the landscape. The winds blow clouds in and out, stir up the dust, and sometimes blow debris about. At times, we find new things have landed in our gardens and call our attention to start to clear away what winter has left behind.

With the children, we recite a verse while walking in a circle, contracting (with the little winds) and expanding (with the big winds):

The little winds they whisper, they whisper as they pass,

Telling all their secrets to the flowers and the grass.

How do you stay grounded when winds of change are blowing?

The big winds, they bluster, they bluster all about.

The little winds they whisper, but the big winds shout!

Yes, the winds have their say in springtime. It can take a lot of energy to stay warm, to stay grounded and centered when it is windy. When we are transitioning from one season to the next, the wind can wake us up and remind us that change is happening. The energy of the wind, the energy of transitions can feel a bit chaotic while we wonder what might blow our way or blow us away. But when we pull our coats close, look toward the ground and forge ahead in spite of the resistance, we might take a turn and find the wind on our backs!

When we combine the blue of the water with the golden yellow of the sunshine, we find beautiful shades of green. That is the color of springtime, of renewal, of our heart forces. "Love will come again like wheat that springeth green."

Joy springs up in our hearts when we experience spring's renewal. Hope and love surge. We find ourselves grateful for the beauty of spring and for the glory of creation and for the creator. After the months of sleep, nature is reawakened and so are we! We celebrate the water, the earth, the sky, and the sun. Look at all they have done!

It is in the gesture of hearts opening and the swell of joy in springtime that we find ourselves, each other, and all that is heavenly. Nature nourishes us and gives us strength. We have weathered the winter months and kept the light kindled in our hearts. We now celebrate that nature has brought the sunlight and the rain back to us and with it the green earth.

Do you see signs of renewal in your mind, body and soul?

FIFTH MARCH WEEK

Besides sensory forces of nature that sustain us, there are invisible but palpable emotional forces amongst humans and invisible divine forces above, below, before and behind us. Guardian angels weave a mantle of love all around us. They are never closer than when we are young children.

The 19th century painter, Thomas Cole, painted a series representing a voyager traveling in a boat though the stages of life. In each stage, the scenery and the role of the person in relationship to the boat and to the angel shift. It's a powerful depiction of this personal yet universal relationship.

If we came from a heavenly place before descending to earth, perhaps our relationship to angelic beings is already forged; we just need to remember and to connect with it. A heavenly imprint lives in our souls as a light we carry within us lifelong.

Do you connect with the divine in yourself and others?

It's easy to imagine that we descend from heavenly realms when we look at an infant who comes, according to poet William Wordsworth, "trailing clouds of glory." From heavenly realms, we come to live for a time on Earth but we are not alone. Here we are woven into an interconnected web of nature, humanity and the divine that supports us so that in our lifetimes we can live out the imprint of our destiny.

Just as children evolve in consciousness as they grow up, so does humanity grow and evolve, entering new states of consciousness that extend over long periods of time or epochs. Things that were once seen and understood with ease earlier in the evolution of the human being are no longer apparent to us. We need to develop the eyes to see them and to understand supersensible phenomena, or information that exists beyond our senses.

In order to develop eyes that can see beyond what the senses provide, we need to acknowledge that there is always more than meets the eye. Being in the presence of children helps us to enter this world. Children are at ease with unseen phenomenon; their consciousness has not yet evolved to the point of forgetting the secrets of the heavens and earth.

They delight in stories of angels and elves, fairies and gnomes, and might glimpse them, especially if they have been introduced through art and stories.

As they grow, children will lose this consciousness and it is right that it is so. But a lingering memory will remain.

They might sense that they are held by other than earthly beings and trust that they are supported as they wind through this earthly maze. Humans are hardwired for this struggle and what comes along provides opportunities for learning.

Rudolf Steiner said, "[Experience] comes from a world directive full of wisdom." Let that wisdom be our guide and trust that whatever we need will come to us so we can continue to grow and evolve in consciousness.

How do you acknowledge what you cannot yet see?

Spring awakens the senses and heart forces. It is often compared to falling in love. There is a quality to the return of the sun's warmth and the plant world that calls for our attention and we see them anew.

When entering nature, it begs us to observe and experience what is there. There is a life force flowing through the elements, the plants and all creatures. Can you experience it as well as your own life force? What enlivens it? We know that children are well served by rhythm, repetition and reverence when they are developing their physical bodies and gestating their etheric bodies or life force, but there is a more universal application. These tenets can be called upon to strengthen life force at any age.

Consider your life's rhythms

What practices enliven your life force?

regarding eating, sleeping, exercising and recreating, and any other habit you have. Look for a healthy balance in them. There is a power to repetition, are you aware of the things you are inwardly repeating to yourself? What are the mantras or phrases that reoccur in your ongoing inner dialogue? Gratitude is a powerful one; a practice of saying thank you can strengthen us, putting our focus on what is positive in our lives.

Finally, pay attention to what you revere. To revere is to take in something wholeheartedly, awakening our heart forces. You are deeply connected to whatever you revere. Is it worthy? These are the things that will enliven us or increase our life force if we engage in them, whatever our circumstances might be.

Imagine the journey of a child to adult consciousness. After growing in a watery, protected environment for about nine months, there is a transition after which the child wakes up in the physical world. Neural connections have already formed in utero and continue to be made based on the sensory environment the child encounters. These connections become the child's framework for how the world works; those experiences that are repeated become the stories most strongly held as reality, regardless of additional information that might contradict them.

During each stage of human development, there is a time when the development of each of the four bodies is emphasized. In the first seven-year period the child's physical body continues to develop, supported by the sculpting forces of the energy body;

Are you aware of how you have evolved and are evolving?

then a period when the astral or soul body is birthed, and finally the ego body which is our individual spiritual self, capable of higher level thinking. Our lives continue in seven-year stages. This is the archetype of human development, but real lives do not match the archetype; humans are unique. Fortunately, there is always the opportunity to make conscious what has been unconsciously impacting our lives and to create new stories to replace old ones that are not serving us. Working with the substance of our lives, we become aware, accepting and able to digest whatever is coming to us. When our thoughts, feelings and actions are integrated, we have achieved a level of functioning that leads to health, happiness and wholeness. It is a dynamic process of evolution.

Springtime is the morning of the year when nature experiences rapid growth after winter's rest. It is a time of preparation, of getting the garden ready, just as in early childhood, we prepare for the developing self to grow. We slowly awaken to the world and to ourselves in it. Mornings are special times; they set the tone for what follows, just as early childhood can set the tone for a person's life.

Become aware of how you get up in the morning and consider whether your habits serve you. Do you wake up stretching and sensing how your body feels and noticing your first thoughts of the day? If it's a stressful time of day for you, are you aware of the impact of stress hormones on your system? Many wisdom traditions suggest physical movement to awaken the body; mindfulness meditation, reading or affirmations to awaken the mind; food and drink to recharge the system. There is a wide range of practices or rituals that can be used to guide us in finding the way back into waking consciousness after a night's sleep.

How do you greet the day?

Do you give yourself enough time to do what you have to do in the morning? Is there something you would like to do differently in order to get ready to greet the day? If you need to make changes in your morning routine, begin training yourself now. Experts say that it takes anywhere from 21 to 66 times practicing a new behavior for it to become a habit. If you begin now, new habits can be established long before winter and its sleepy quality returns. With practice and patience, one day you may find your mornings have been made new and the seeds you intentionally plant first thing are growing in your garden throughout the day.

Children learn through imitation; they imitate not only our outward gestures but our inward ones as well. Both our insides and outsides are visible to them; their survival depends on tuning in to those they depend on. They are truth tellers; we cannot hide in their presence, although we may prefer to conceal certain characteristics from others and even from ourselves.

That's being human. What can we do when we recognize something we would like to change in ourselves? Be aware and curious. Strive to accept whatever is, rather than judge or criticize it. Continue to observe yourself with genuine and neutral interest. The act of paying mindful attention to our thoughts, feelings and behaviors without a story (judgments and criticisms are stories based on conditioning) can, in itself, bring about change.

Since integrity is possible in human behavior and perfection is not, that's the one to strive for: being honest with ourselves is where change begins.

Although we cannot always change things in ourselves as quickly as we would like, if we become aware and accept whatever is, we can stay connected to ourselves, to others, and to the possibility of change. It is through our repeated thoughts and stories that we bring our pasts into the future. When we let the stories go, we might see circumstances in a fresh way and then open up to whatever the future brings.

Do you live with integrity?

Mothers and May—they bring to mind creation and all its glory. Although everyone is not a mother, this celebration is universal because everyone has a mother and can engage in mothering practices. We also share our home, often referred to as Mother Earth who takes care of us just as we are the stewards who must take care of her. It's the time of year to acknowledge the practice of mothering. If you hold young children in your care, giving them what they need to grow and develop, you are engaging in this practice.

Mothering involves caring and tending, nurturing and supporting, all the while teaching these arts and impacting society profoundly. Mother Earth provides us with food, air to breathe, and water for drinking and cleansing. Between Mother Earth, our biological mothers, family and colleagues who care, we can get our needs for mothering met no matter what our personal circumstances. With that support, we can care for ourselves, bearing the archetype of mother within so it can flow from us, encircling us with the energy of nurturing.

In the month of May, the tradition of celebrating nature's fertility and the gifts she bestows on us dates back to ancient times.

What is your practice of gratitude?

From this tradition, we practice grace before meals when we thank the earth for all she provides. On Mother's Day, which is a modern tradition, we take time to thank our mothers, but we can increase this energy with a habit of gratitude year round for the one who gave us life, for those who have nurtured us, and for those who continue to do so. As a young child, we depended on this care to survive and with it at any time in our lives, we can not only survive, but heal and thrive. Thanks to all those who nurture children, others and socially uplifting projects. You make our world a warm, loving and beautiful place, as beautiful as the month of May.

Spring is a season of expansion. The sense world draws us outdoors and gives us a feeling of boundlessness. If we go too far, we may end up outside of ourselves, in a way that is ungrounded, for as human beings we live between Heaven and Earth. Our feet are planted on the earth but we are not earth-bound only like plants. We may reach for the sky in our thoughts and dreams without ever reaching its heights.

The power of our humanity lives in our hearts. Our heart forces dwell in the present, taking in what is happening moment to moment, not what we wish would happen. Each moment has potential, although our habits of thinking may lead us to the same conclusions again and again. It is possible to be open and aware without imposing judgment or thought but to be in a way that is independent of the stimulus before us, to experience new and creative thoughts. This way of being takes practice.

Answers to the difficulties we face come from within the direct experience. The more we can observe with neutral awareness what is, the more we can access the wise thinking that comes from our heart forces. It is a blend of thought and emotion; but is independent of each. It is our strength and our majesty, what it is to be truly human; something we may strive for throughout our lives. When we experience glimpses or moments of this wise heart-thinking, we feel connected to ourselves, to others, to the ground under our feet and to the expansiveness of the universe. Then we know it is worth coming back again and again to the practice of being present in the moment.

How do you remain open and present?

56

Fourth May Week

Is there anything more lovely than nature's expression at this time of year? Beholding nature can remind us of our intrinsic capability to create beauty. Humans have an etheric body like the plant world; it is a renewable energy force. It regulates our ability to maintain homeostasis, to take in and assimilate nutrients from food and sensory information from the environment. It is fed by rhythms, equanimity (emotional balance) and positive thinking.

During the first seven years of life, children are filling up their etheric bodies so that the physical body is developed enough to shift the focus from its development to other learning. If a child has experienced enough unrestricted movement and sensory integration to form a balanced network of neural connections evidenced by physical movement, then the child is ready for school.

The etheric body is supported by time outdoors as well as one-pointedness, or doing one thing at a time. It's a good exercise to check in every now and then to see where you are. I often find myself doing one thing and, at the same time, also planning the future or mulling over the past. Divided attention is not an efficient way of functioning. Wandering into the future or the past unconsciously can lead us away from the gift of the moment we are experiencing now. Let nature demonstrate how to show up in the moment, let it renew us, and teach us to let go because everything is ephemeral. Be present to this moment, for it will pass as all things do.

Where are you in your mind, body, and soul right now?

SUMMER

Finding Community

First June Week

Glorious and golden summer days are ahead. We welcome the sunshine and warmth and know that the earth is firm yet ever-changing. While everything is changing and growing, we might feel the urge to hold on, to resist change. We can look toward nature to witness graceful change and quiet acceptance. When we do not resist what comes, discomfort is fleeting. Light in our thinking involves seeing what is, including any discomfort without needing to change, judge or make it go away. Then our thoughts and feelings flow through us like a gentle breeze on a summer day.

Standing still is not an option in this life; even if we want to stay in the same place, it requires growth and adaptation to meet changing circumstances. As summer demonstrates, it is the season to allow light to enter us. When we do, we can find the ground beneath our feet, even as it shifts, and hold our center in the midst of change. Without the light illuminating our thoughts, our thinking can become cloudy, driven by fear of the future or stuck in regrets of the past, even manifesting over time in our physical bodies. We may miss opportunities and not see what is there.

When our thinking is enlightened, we can experience flexibility and freedom.

Striving for lightness and noticing whatever is occurring is an ongoing practice that requires patience and compassion. We tend to prefer predictability and resist change. But by doing so, we are placing our safety and security in outward circumstances. If we maintain a neutral stance, avoiding opinions about likes and dislikes, security can dwell within us, unchanging, as a place we can return to whenever we wander away from it. Possibility lives each moment when we seek the light and embrace change and growth!

Do you seek neutrality or equanimity?

The sun is reaching to its highest height; golden rays are warming the earth. The light penetrates our bodies, souls and spirits. Summer's quality is expansive; it brings us out of our homes and into connections with nature and with other people.

What is more important than that? Many things are urgent and call for our attention, but nothing is as important as our relationship with ourselves and with others. Summer is the time to nurture connections much like we nurture plants in the garden. We tend relationships by weeding out what does not serve, by watering them with loving hearts, and by celebrating their growth and beauty. It is through our connections with others that we can see ourselves, both our highest Selves and the weed-like habits that we want to remove from our gardens.

How do you shape the will while nurturing the spirit?

While children are developing their will forces, they have of lots of enthusiasm and energy for doing things. How do we encourage them to do what needs to be done to shape their will forces? We do not engage in harsh or unkind measures because this activates the child's resistance; rather with our warm spirits, we honor the children's spirits while guiding them. Although children's bodies are small and they are early in their developmental journey, their spirits are big just like ours. In order to support their development, we build a bond of good will that allows children to learn through imitating us. If we dishonor the spirit of the child, trauma occurs and the imitative mode of learning is broken; then we must work to repair it.

THIRD JUNE WEEK

Summer reaches its fullest expression when the sun is at its highest point in the sky and we celebrate the longest day of the year, the summer solstice. The roses and peonies are in full bloom and our senses are filled with their glory. Activity of the fairies is heightened, as memorialized in Shakespeare's play, *A Midsummer Night's Dream.*

Just as individuals have one element that is most pronounced in their temperament, so do the seasons. It is easy to imagine that the fire element is summer's. The energy is upward and expansive as demonstrated by plants that are put in the earth in the spring to grow upward in the warmth of the summer sun. The sunflower, for example, is an expression of summer and its fire element.

Summer's gifts include: warmth, joy, laughter, partnership, equal sharing, love, relationship and compassion, to name a few. In order to fully embrace the quality of summer, we are encouraged to take in the longer hours of sunlight by getting up early and staying up a little later. It is the time for activity: bicycling, boating and hiking, often in the company of family and friends. Enjoying the sun, the water, and the ease in outdoor movement call to us in summer, and it's important to answer the call of the season! It is the time of year for gathering outdoors perhaps around a fire, sharing stories and connecting with others, gazing into the sky with hopes of spotting a falling star or firefly flitting through the air. Although some of us may not need encouragement to do so, it is validating to hear summer is the time to be playful, to have fun, and live passionately.

How does summer bring out your sense of play, fun, and passion?

At the summer solstice, we find ourselves in the world devoted to what is beyond ourselves. The expansion in nature brings us out of the personal Self into a World or cosmic Self, connected to all that is. When we flow with the wisdom of nature at this time of year, we experience the fullness of our divinity. Matters that affect our small Self are diminished in the context of the greater world that we experience, revealed in the light of the sun and human consciousness.

When we expand and contract along with the cycles of nature, we are in sync or flowing with the world and what lies beyond our personal selves. Summer calls us out, with its fullest expression on the solstice or June 21st. Celebrating nature in community gives us a template for our collective humanity and provides a context for our experiences and our inner yearnings. While we celebrate the sun and what is divinely expressed in us, we are also beginning the process of going inward. At this time of year, we are encouraged to take the experience of our Self, acknowledge it, and begin letting go of any attachment to it—all at the same time. Nature provides a template for balance that prevents us from experiencing extremes; just as we are the most expanded into the world, the energy shifts inward.

The golden sun has reached its peak; now ends the earth's expansion or outbreath. The counter movement is an inhalation or in-breath that leads us slowly but surely to the winter solstice and the shortest day of the year, the peak of inwardness for humankind. Through the course of the year, there is a balance of breathing in and breathing out that occurs with such subtlety that it may not be obvious unless we are paying attention to it. Notice what is happening in the world and within your Self. At the time of the solstice, we may ask ourselves to recognize our divine purpose and how we are connected to it, to take what has been revealed to us into our inner life so that what lives in the outer expression of the world can also live deeply within us.

How do you find your Self in community at the summer solstice?

Fifth June Week

While we drink in nature's rich gifts, our senses are enlivened. The earth is bestowing its bounty upon us and our hearts open up in gratitude. At the same time that we experience the greatness of the earth, we might long to connect with the heavenly ranks where the angels live.

This longing for the spirit fulfills something that lives within our souls, just as we are linked with nature through our physical bodies. This time of year when we are open to receiving, we may seek the wise and powerful beings of the heavens. In our human experience, we are grounded on the earth, with a tendency to look upward toward the heavens. Where can we find balance?

What does balance look like during summer's peak?

If we pay attention within our hearts and minds, we might hear contrasting voices speaking to us, voices that can throw us out of balance: a voice that leads us to that which is kind, generous, and loving within us and voice of fear that motivates us to protect ourselves, hold onto what we have, and assume ill intentions on the part of others. These voices are nourished by our attention. Our lives grow full of love or fear, depending on which voice we feed. Pay attention. Listen and nourish the voice that leads you to the life of your choice, to live the life of your dreams.

At the same time that we are called to engage with the earth's expression in summer, our eyes are drawn upward. Fireworks evoke awe with their displays of color and sound, and when the smoke dissipates, our eyes may continue focusing upward, taking in the spectacle of the evening sky in summer.

There is much wonder to find there and to awaken our souls to the eternal. Our sense of time and distance is expanded when we gaze toward the sparkling dome above us. Humans are both cosmic, light-filled beings and earth-bound, held by the forces of gravity. The sky is our link to the heavens. While gazing at the sky over the course of days, weeks and months, movement of the planets and stars may capture our attention. We may identify constellations and see patterns that occur over the course of the year, acknowledging rhythms that govern celestial movement.

Rudolf Steiner said, "When we observe the life of the world of stars, we are beholding the bodies of the Gods and, ultimately, of Divinity Itself." The same forces that shaped the heavenly sky shaped the human being. Experiencing the sky above gives us a sense of our oneness with the universe. In this cosmic perspective, in the timeframe of the eternal, there is no need to hurry or to force solutions, but there is a call to awaken to the spark of divinity that lives within us. It is where the practical meets the spiritual that we find our full expression of humanity.

Do you gaze at the night sky?

Where do we find strength when we need it to meet life's challenges? The sun's light is warm and bright; it wraps around us. It sparkles on the water and streams through the air. Even in the dense forest, light finds a way through the canopy of leaves to create a play of light and shadow. But beyond the physical, there are other forces that serve us and give us strength: spiritual forces, angelic forces that await our appeal before they provide support. They surround children with invisible protection, and as we age, they step back with respect for our free will, coming to our aid only when we ask for it. Can you sense their support? Can you imagine that there is more than what can be seen in this world, that there are forces that live beyond this visible veil of light?

How do you engage with spiritual forces?

We may be strengthened by unseen forces that come to our aid, to support our work with the children. There is a unique and visceral quality to an environment that is carefully constructed for children's safety and healthy development in which there is also a relationship cultivated to that which is sacred, that which is of the spirit. Let the light of earthly and other worldly forces shine into us, and give us strength.

The world shines into us through our senses. Summer provides many sensory gifts; they enter our bodies, and when they fall on fertile ground, they ripen within us. Where do the fruits of the Sun, the grace, the glorious light find a home in the human body?

They dwell in our hearts, the center of courage and gracefulness. The human heart performs much more than a physical task, and building a home for powerful soul forces takes care, skill and artfulness. It takes willingness to experience what is, to stay open to the broad range of feelings that flow through us, and to practice compassion toward ourselves and others.

Do you differentiate the transient from the eternal?

At times, we will experience pain and sorrow; there is a time for everything in this life. If we resist the pains of living, we increase the suffering. When we allow both life's joys and sorrows to be without resisting them, they flow through us, and the kernel of wisdom acquired, like a precious pearl, then lives on in our hearts.

Let your heart be strong, be open and nonresistant so to be protected from unnecessary struggle. In this way, we focus on the eternal and, when the time comes, let go of that which is transient.

Most adults have a list of things to do and often measure success based on what's been accomplished. A good day is when everything is checked off the list, but at times, there might be a sense of dissatisfaction in spite of that accomplishment. Consider that there is more to life than doing.

The will is only one aspect of our humanity. Equally important are the how and the emotional quality that we bring to our actions. Children take in the emotional quality of our words and actions even more than the content. When we say kind words in an angry voice or gesture, it is the anger that will leave the greater impact.

How can you bring joy and love to your words and actions? Consider spreading love as a goal while making a list of things to do. Can I do this with joy or love? If not, can I afford not to do this? The answer will vary and we often find that by pausing and

How do you cultivate love and joy in your deeds?

choosing, we can dig deeper and find more within us than we thought we could. According to the law of karma, we receive what we give. Notice how it feels to receive what is given with joy and love. Notice how it feels to imbue your actions with the intention of joy and love. How does this impact your feeling of satisfaction?

It is a practice, one that we may never achieve perfection in doing, but one that is worth striving for. The more we practice bringing joy and love to our actions, encounters and inward sentiments, the more we will be able to access it. Even if our practices are not conscious, we do have habits of how we do things, for example, negativity is a habit that is strengthened through practice. Take a look at the things you do and the practice of how you do them; notice what they bring to you in your life.

There is a subtle change in the light when August comes. The sound of the cicadas seems to say summer is coming to an end, the season is changing. With that awareness comes a quiet call to inward action. The warmth and light we have enjoyed needs a home in our hearts to carry us through the seasons ahead; it's time to start building that home.

How do we build a sacred space within our hearts for the Sun to dwell? It is through our heartfelt striving to love one another that we make this home within us. Courage and compassion drive us to connect with ourselves and with each other; that connection is the expression of love. To connect in an authentic way requires vulnerability, the feeling of being open and exposed, which can be uncomfortable. Discomfort is a normal part of the process of growth. Just as our heart provides a safe space for the light, our community can provide a safe place for us to strive, at times to fail, and to continue striving. Connecting with the perfect Light we hold in our hearts inspires us to strive, to forgive, to accept and to connect. We can allow ourselves to be seen by others in this journey for it is a shared one, a human one. That's how we grow.

Let nature lead us to build a home for the light of love in our hearts and our community to support us on the way. We may not see progress every day, but over time we will find that our work and our relationships are imbued with a love that is growing, that we are connecting with others in an authentic way, and that our lives are enriched by it.

How do you create a home for the light in your life?

We remember the summer solstice when the pull outward into the world reached its peak, after which began the gradual inward-turning process. This expansion and contraction is the earth's breathing out and breathing in, and it affects us on a physical and soul level, too. It is so slow and gentle that we do not notice it happening until the end of summer, when we know for certain that the light has changed.

We are not meant to find our way alone; we are meant to care about and for one another. If we stayed separate and alone, we would experience only fear. In the expansiveness of summer, it is easy to find one another and every tree, star and flower in nature. Nature calls us out into it. When love calls us out into the world, we find the gifts of nature and our shared humanity.

How do you connect with others?

The bridge between humans is love. It connects us and it is a practice rather than a feeling.

Love can conquer loneliness and fear; it can bring healing to our hearts, minds and bodies. We are not alone. With love, we can stay connected. Even while the earth is breathing in, slowly contracting, we can reach out to find one another.

When we experience the summer sun, its warmth brings power to humankind. Like plants in nature, in the summertime, seeds ripen in our souls.

What seeds did we plant in the spring? We may not recognize them because they are not packaged like seeds we purchase for the flower or vegetable garden. We plant seeds with our every thought and deed. They grow in the garden of our souls. The fiery strength of summer impacts life forces outside and within us.

We have been warmed by the sun. Our will forces are strengthened. By tending the ripening seeds within us, we prepare to receive the harvest in our lives. What grew from the outside in will continue to grow from the inside out. Choose the seeds you plant and tend in your soul with care, for something is growing. And our lives provide a mirror for what is growing inside us.

What seeds have grown in your soul?

Fourth August Week

The light at summer's end continues to shower us with warmth. Nature is delivering ripened fruits that are delicious and sweet. Meteor showers rain iron down from the sky, lending heavenly strength to human endeavors. Our hearts and bodies are strengthened.

When we grow strong within, we can become quiet. It is a practice that we learn by doing. In the quiet, we experience whatever is, without judgment or resistance. Equanimity is allowing everything to be and flow through us. It creates a fertile ground that nourishes the seeds within us, helping them to grow. Nature does not resist what comes; it adapts to it.

With summer's expansive activity coming to an end, take time to pause and find the quiet. Listen within. When we connect to our souls with compassion, we can connect with others as well. Our courage is supported; forces that are greater than us rejoice when we are brave in spite of discomfort. Listen, commit to the practice and await the harvest. It will come.

Do you pause to sit and listen?

*N*ow you have completed a year of self-development. Congratulations! Take a moment to acknowledge what you have done. You can go back next year and start again, reading the excerpts week by week. Since you have grown, you will experience the readings anew and find new answers to the questions.

You may also choose to approach the book in a novel way by looking in the table of contents and picking a question, then reading the excerpt. Whatever way you use the book is the right way to use it.

By all means, make it your own and enjoy finding answers to the questions and getting to know your Self as a teacher and a student throughout the seasons.